THE WINE AND WISDOM SERIES No.5

MOTIVATION

A One Act Play

Lynn Brittney

Published by Playstage
United Kingdom.

An imprint of Write Publications Ltd

www.playsforadults.com

Designed by Kate Lowe, Greensands Graphics
Printed by Creeds Ltd, Bridport, Dorset

Note to producers about staging "Motivation"

The action of the play takes place in a room in a large bank, therefore the décor should have a feeling of corporate blandness about it – perhaps metal framed chairs with grey upholstery, coffee table, one wall where the top half is glass etc.

The seating should be laid out in a semi circle around a large central coffee table. There should be five, not four chairs, to enable MEL to go over and comfort DORIS when she cries. Thus, the chair between ETHAN and DORIS should be empty.

Set dressing could include sales charts on the wall; a mocked-up savings package poster etc. (Do not use any high street bank posters in case an organisation should take offence at the content of the play!)

The uniform of the staff is important. Everyone should wear the same colour suit – jacket and skirt for the women, jacket and trousers for the men. The women's patterned blouses should match and the men's shirt's should be in a plain but toning colour. If possible the men could have ties made from the same material as the women's blouses. If this is not possible, then ties in the same colour as their suits. This is all to suggest corporate uniformity.

Try not to make the action too static. Although PATRICK comes and goes and MEL changes seats, the cast are seated for a large part of the play. Therefore, you need to create movement such as picking up and putting down coffee cups on the table; changing position to write notes; using their hands expressively when speaking and so on. Body language is quite important. PATRICK is lazy and therefore would sprawl in his chair; ETHAN is young and restless, so he would probably fidget a lot; MEL is very self-contained but relaxed and DORIS is feeling threatened but at the same time is a very organised woman, so she would sit bolt upright and not cross her legs. In this way you can create a realistic impression of the characters in the play.

WINE AND WISDOM 5 : MOTIVATION

CAST *(In order of appearance)*

DORIS   very organised and efficient, aged 50+

MEL   self assured and ambitious, aged 25-30

ETHAN   teenager, a bit dim, sports mad, aged 17 – 19

PATRICK   laid back, lazy, charming, aged 50+

2 female and 2 male parts.

The action takes place in a meeting room in a bank.

WINE AND WISDOM 5
MOTIVATION

A meeting room in the head office of a large bank. There are five occasional chairs and a low table between each of them (making four in total). They are arranged in a semi-circle, facing the audience. On the back wall is a filing cabinet with a potted plant on top. There is a Sales Graph on the wall, which says: "SALES FOR THE MONTH OF JUNE". DORIS enters, carrying a file, some quiz books and she has a polystyrene cup of coffee in her hand. She is followed by MEL, who carries a large notepad. They are both dressed in an identical uniform of the same coloured jacket, skirt and patterned blouse. They have name tags on their lapels. DORIS is irritable and MEL is aware of her mood.

DORIS   I still don't know why Mr Jenkins took it into his head that I needed help with the quiz night. I've organized it for the last ten years and I've never needed any help before.

MEL   Perhaps he just felt that you ought to share the load a bit. I mean now that you're approaching retirement.

DORIS   I'm only fifty three and I am not senile!

MEL   I'm sure no-one thinks you are, Doris. It's just that you are one of the candidates for the early retirement package and someone else needs to know how to run the quiz night, in case you do decide to take up the offer.

DORIS   Well I won't and I've told him so. But he never listens to me. I can understand me sharing my experience with one person but a committee? That's just foolishness. Everyone knows that it takes twice as long to put something together when a committee is involved.

MEL   Mr Jenkins called it a "work team" not a committee. We're supposed to help you. Not do the thing instead of you.

DORIS   *(slightly mollified)* Well, I just hope that people do realize that they are here to assist me and not interfere.

MEL   I'm sure they do.

DORIS   And the very least they can do is be on time! Where are the men, for goodness sake?

MEL   I saw Ethan going into the canteen. He said he was just going to get a coffee and he would be right along.

DORIS   Hmm. And Patrick?

MEL   Don't know.

DORIS   Anyway, I don't expect much input from either of those two. If Ethan had a thought it would die of loneliness and Patrick tries very hard not to think – it's too tiring for him.

MEL   *(smiling)* That's a pretty accurate assessment.

(ETHAN shambles in with a polystyrene cup of coffee. He has no notepad or pen. He is wearing the male version of the uniform – matching jacket and trousers, plain shirt and a tie, which matches the pattern on the women's blouses.)

ETHAN   Am I late?

DORIS   Yes you are. We've only got the staff-training hour, before the tills open up. We can't afford to sit around wasting time.

ETHAN   Sorry.

(PATRICK enters. He is also wearing the uniform but he

has the top button of his shirt open and his tie pulled down.
His name tag is missing. He is an attractive man but
everything about him – his dress, his body language –
suggests laziness.)

PATRICK   Bit of a lark, this, isn't it?

DORIS   What? You being late? I don't think so.

PATRICK   Am I? Sorry old girl. No, I mean, getting to do this quiz
            thing instead of the usual training malarkey.

DORIS   I'm sure that you welcome any opportunity to get out of
            serious work Patrick, but I'm afraid I regard the creation of
            the company Quiz Night as very hard work indeed.

PATRICK   Surely not? Bunging a few questions together? Can't be all
            that hard.

DORIS   *(sighing)* What's the point – let's just get started shall we?

            (Everyone sits down except PATRICK.)

PATRICK   That's a good idea. Coffee. You start without me, I'll just go
            and get myself a cup. *(PATRICK exits.)*

DORIS   Like I said. What is the point?

MEL   Well, we can make a start, can't we? I've got a notepad.

ETHAN   Oh. I didn't bring anything. Sorry.

MEL   Here. Have a piece of mine. *(She tears off a few sheets and
            hands it to him)* Have you got something to write with?

            (ETHAN shakes his head.)

DORIS   Well really! Here, have a pen! *(She opens up a file to reveal
            several pens neatly clipped into the front. She removes one
            and gives it to him.)* Now. As you know, the Quiz Night is
            a very important part of our corporate social calendar.

Every year, the bank chooses a charity to benefit from the money raised by the Quiz Night. This year it is to be the local hospice...

MEL   Oh good.

DORIS   Yes. We get some very good publicity out of this. This will be our eleventh year and we need to make sure that the event is as enjoyable as all the previous years have been.

ETHAN   Eleven years! God!

DORIS   Right. I've selected all the usual categories for the ten rounds of questions. Perhaps you'd like to write them down.

(ETHAN and MEL sit with pens poised.)

DORIS   Round one – General Knowledge. We always have this first, as a warm-up round. It seems to sort out the men from the boys, so to speak, so we get a clear indication, by round two, which teams are forging ahead. Round two – Sport.

ETHAN   Good.

DORIS   Mr Jenkins insists on a sport round, for the benefit of the male staff, who are usually lagging behind a bit after the general knowledge round. Round three – British History. Always a tough one and, obviously getting tougher, as I try never to repeat questions from previous years. However, as most of the staff , now, have only been with us about five years, I think we could take a chance and repeat the questions on British history from ten years ago. So I've photocopied them for you. *(DORIS unclips two photocopied sheets from her file and hands them to the other two.)*

It goes without saying that these questions are absolutely confidential and, therefore, when you have read them, I would like them back please. We don't want them falling into the wrong hands before the actual night.

ETHAN   Like exam papers, eh?

DORIS   Exactly. Now, round four is Food.....

MEL   Sorry, can I just interrupt you a moment?

DORIS   If you must.

MEL   Well, this round on British History. I'm wondering if it's entirely suitable.

DORIS   Why would it not be suitable?

MEL   Well, because over forty percent of our head office staff are not British, that's why. We have a large number of Asian and Afro-Caribbean employees now.

DORIS   Do they not study British History?

MEL   Why would they?

DORIS   Because they used to be part of the British Empire. I assume that they still learn about Britain in their schools.

MEL   I think you'll find that they concentrate more on their own cultural background nowadays.

ETHAN   I wouldn't know the answers to any of these questions myself.

DORIS   Ethan dear...without wishing to be rude... I hardly think that your level of intellect is what we should be basing this quiz on.

ETHAN   *(to MEL)* Did she just insult me?

MEL   In the nicest possible way, Ethan. Forget about it.

ETHAN   *(unsure)* If you say so.

MEL   The thing is, Doris. Your generation had quite a different education to our generation.

DORIS   I know dear. It was very much better.

MEL   *(trying to be patient)* Well that's as may be…but most of the staff in this bank are *my* generation. At the present time, sixty seven percent of our employees are under the age of thirty five.

DORIS   *(irritated)* Please don't quote Human Resources statistics at me. I am quite aware that I am surrounded by people who are half my age. Only *too* aware.

(PATRICK returns with a cup of coffee and a large Danish pastry, which he starts to eat.)

PATRICK   Sorry about that. Had to have some breakfast. Didn't have time this morning.

DORIS   You should make time. It's the most important meal of the day.

PATRICK   Thanks but I'd rather have an extra hour's sleep. So, where are we?

MEL   We are just debating the value of having a round on British History when a large percentage of our staff is not British.

PATRICK   Right. Good point. Hate history anyway.

DORIS   *(accepting defeat but not liking it)* Fine. We'll drop British History.

MEL   What shall we put in its place?

DORIS   I'd rather discuss that after we have been through all the rounds, if you don't mind Mel.

MEL	OK, you're in charge.
DORIS	*(firmly)* Yes. Round four – Food.
PATRICK	Excellent. One subject I know about.
MEL	Is it actually about cookery?
DORIS	How do you mean? Recipes and cookery terms and the like?
MEL	Yes.
DORIS	There are a certain proportion of the questions that relate to cookery terms, yes.
MEL	*(looking doubtful)* Mmmm.
DORIS	*(getting exasperated)* What is the problem now? Are you going to tell me that your generation doesn't know anything about cooking?
MEL	Well, basically, yes, I'm afraid. Microwaves, you see. Ready meals. Don't teach cookery in schools and so on.
DORIS	Mel, there are wall-to-wall cookery programmes on television! There are magazines on sale every month about cookery! How can they not know how to cook?!
MEL	I know there are TV programmes and magazines but they are all aimed at the forty to sixty age group. Have you seen the adverts in the magazines?
PATRICK	What? Chair lifts and incontinence pads? *(He sniggers)*
DORIS	*(annoyed)* Oh really!
MEL	No, no. Not that extreme. No, they're for middle-aged fashion catalogues, cruises, insurance, stuff like that.
DORIS	So are you saying that we throw out the Food round now?

MEL	No, not at all. I'm just saying that we should be careful about the questions.
DORIS	Could you give me an example?
MEL	Well, we could have a question like "What type of pizza is formaggio?" Everyone knows the different types of pizzas. Or we could have one like "What strength is a Balti Curry? Is it Medium, Hot or Very Hot?" Stuff like that. Wait a minute....*(getting very excited)...* we should make all the question multiple choice!
ETHAN	Good idea. I like having the options.
DORIS	*(sarcastically)* In other words, dear, you are suggesting that we "dumb down" the whole quiz to cater for the under thirty year olds who have never been taught to have an original thought.
PATRICK	*(mock horror)* Oh, oh! Doris is getting sarcastic. Now you've done it Mel.
MEL	*(gritting her teeth)* Look. I get really pissed off with people who keep saying that everything nowadays is "dumbed-down". I worked bloody hard to get my A levels and I worked bloody hard to get a decent degree at uni. I don't think anything that I did was "dumbed-down". That's just a crap argument used by people who are basically jealous of young people doing their best in life.
ETHAN	Too right. I failed my A levels, personally, but I'm with you all the way.
PATRICK	Look, there's no point in arguing about all of this. It's only a quiz night.
DORIS	*(dismissive)* That's typical. When do you ever think

anything is important, Patrick?

PATRICK   *(refusing to be baited)* No, no. It's alright. You can have a go at me, if you like, Doris. I know I'm a lazy bugger. I just work to pay the bills. I'm not a company animal through and through, like you. But it is just a quiz. A bit of fun. A charity event. The more money we raise, the better the bank looks. So, if you have to cut the old cloth a bit to accommodate the youngsters, so what? Relax about it, Doris. Eh? Eh?

DORIS   *(accepting that she is outnumbered and feeling a little crushed)* Yes. I suppose you're right. I do take these things a bit too seriously. It's a good idea to rework the Food round. *(Rallying some of her spirit a little)* But I do reject the multiple-choice idea. That makes things too easy.

MEL   *(sulking a little)* If you say so. But it's what they do on all the television quizzes.

DORIS   I know but we don't have to slavishly follow television trends, do we?

ETHAN   Hey, that'd be good! Get the old company to do a "Big Brother". They could lock a load of employees in a room and we could all watch them on close-circuit TV! Then we could vote to get them chucked out.

PATRICK   *(smiling)* How do you know they're not doing that right now? *(There is a pause while everyone looks unnerved. PATRICK smiles and winds them up further)* I mean, how do you know that we weren't sent into this room as some sort of management test? Perhaps old Jenkins wants to see if we'll tear each other to bits or whether we'll emerge as a unified whole.

DORIS	*(unsure)* Don't be silly. Mr Jenkins wouldn't do a thing like that.
PATRICK	*(enjoying himself)* Ah, you don't know. Why did he suddenly say that the quiz night had to be run by a team, when you have done it successfully on your own for a whole decade? Is it because he thinks you need help Doris? That you can't handle it anymore?
MEL	*(sharply)* Come on Patrick, that's wicked.
PATRICK	*(refusing to let go)* Or is it that he's looking to promote someone and he wants to see who will emerge from this room as the true team leader? *(He looks pointedly at MEL; DORIS looks anxiously at MEL and MEL looks at her notepad.)*
MEL	*(uncomfortably)* You're just winding everybody up.
PATRICK	*(still persisting)* Or conversely, perhaps he's trying to weed out some dead wood and those who do not contribute to the exercise will be given their cards?
DORIS	*(triumphant)* Well, you'll be the first one on that list!
PATRICK	*(smiling)* No I won't because Jenkins knows that I have decided to accept the early retirement package. Perhaps it will be you, Doris. Or maybe our sporty young friend here. It won't be Mel because she's fast-tracking up to management.
DORIS	*(looking at MEL)* Is she?
PATRICK	Of course she is. She's on the graduate programme.
MEL	*(feeling awkward)* Patrick, this is nonsense. Shut up and let us get on with this.
PATRICK	*(provocatively finishing his argument)* I shall say no more. I have just thrown my thoughts into the centre of the room. I

shall let them hang there and permeate the gathering.

ETHAN   *(all of this has gone straight over his head)* What does 'permeate' mean?

MEL   Infiltrate or be absorbed into.

ETHAN   *(none the wiser)* Oh. Can I do the questions for the Sport round?

DORIS   *(looking nonplussed at the sudden change of direction)* Er...yes. Why not. Ten questions about Sport. No multiple choice. OK?

ETHAN   Yeah. Good. I'll do them tonight.

DORIS   Now. Round five – quotations. This is sayings by famous people. Is everyone alright with that?

MEL   Well, we come back to the same thing. Are they all quotes from people in history or are there some quotes from living people too? You know, like celebrities.

DORIS   *(acidly)* Do celebrities say anything memorable?

MEL   Well, yeah. Um.. we could have a quote from the Prime Minister...

PATRICK   Like what? "It was nothing to do with me," or "I didn't see any report until yesterday". That could apply to most of the Cabinet.

DORIS   Exactly. Anyway, the Prime Minister is not a celebrity. The description 'celebrity' usually applies to someone with no brain, very little talent...

ETHAN   *(smiling)* And big tits.

DORIS   *(unfazed)* I was going to say, lots of glamour and money, but Ethan's comment is probably just as valid.

MEL	*(being persistent)* Now, I know you don't want to hear this but this is exactly the round where multiple choice would be valuable.
	(DORIS sighs)
	No. Hear me out. You could make it fun as well. For example you could call the round "Who is most likely to say...?" The questions would go something like, "Who would be most likely to say.... "Basically I'm a very shy person." Is it Jordan *(ETHAN laughs and so does PATRICK)*, J.K.Rowling or Russell Brand?
ETHAN	Yeah. I get it. That's good.
DORIS	*(smiling for once)* Actually, that is quite good. I can see how that might work. *(Stubbornly)* But we're not going to apply multiple choice to every round.
MEL	No. OK. But you can see how it might work, can't you?
DORIS	Yes. So, that can be one of your rounds to compile then, as it was your idea.
MEL	Fine.
DORIS	I do, at last feel as though we're getting somewhere.
PATRICK	I need another cup of coffee. Anyone else want one?
ETHAN	Yes. I wouldn't mind one.
MEL	Actually, could you get me a bottle of mineral water? I'll give you the money later.
PATRICK	Fine. Doris?
DORIS	I've got one here but I think it's probably cold now. Go on then. I'll have another one.
PATRICK	Shan't be long. *(PATRICK exits.)*

DORIS   *(worried)* Do you think he's right about this being a
             management test?

MEL   Dunno. When I worked for Human Resources they sent me
             on a course where they taught us about various exercises
             for team building. This scenario is similar to one of those.

DORIS   But why would they do such a thing?

MEL   Like Patrick said, they could be seeing which one of us is
             ripe for promotion or whether any of us are not capable of
             working as a team. There are various reasons.

ETHAN   Well I don't have any problem with team work. I've played
             sport all my life. That's all about team work. I only joined
             this bank because they had such a good sports club.

MEL   *(matter-of-factly to ETHAN)* Of course you know that
             they're closing it.

ETHAN   *(devastated)* What!

MEL   Yes. I'm working in Premises now and they're planning to
             sell off the sports ground.

ETHAN   *(slumping forward and holding his head in his hands)* Shit!
             They can't do that! We're all set to win the cup this year!

MEL   Well, they won't do it for a couple of years but it's on the
             cards. Haven't you heard? I mean everyone knows.

DORIS   *I* didn't know and I think it's a great shame. Not that I use
             the ground that much but I have played the odd game of
             tennis there and it's a lovely venue for staff parties.

MEL   Yes but that's the problem. The bottom line is that nobody
             uses the ground very much...

ETHAN   It's busy every weekend! There's the rugby, football and cricket teams. There's women's hockey and the tennis. How can they say it's not being used enough?

MEL   But, Ethan, how many of those people who use the ground are actually employees? Be honest.

ETHAN   Well. Ok. There's probably five, maybe six people on our team that come from outside. But still…

MEL   See? Over fifty percent of the people using the facility are nothing to do with the bank. It's not cost effective and that's what it's all about.

ETHAN   *(really upset)* Oh man! Oh Jesus! What's the point eh? I might as well leave. We've got a great bunch of lads and now we're going to be homeless.

DORIS   *(bitterly)* It's always about the bottom line, isn't it? Whether it's getting rid of leisure facilities or people, it's always about cost-effectiveness, not about people's morale or well-being.

MEL   But Doris, modern business has to survive. It's a dog eat dog world.

DORIS   How much profit did this bank make last year? Two point seven billion? And they can't let Ethan play sport or let older employees stay in work.

MEL   *(lecturing)* The profit goes to the shareholders and they don't want to share their profit with uneconomic sports clubs or expensive older employees.

DORIS   How am I more expensive than you?

MEL   Because older employees are more inflexible.

DORIS   I am not! I'm willing to do anything! I've been moved twice in the last two years to different departments.

MEL   I know but you don't want to drop everything and move to Sunderland at a moment's notice, do you?

DORIS   *(defensive)* Well, I can't! I've got my house and my friends and everything here!

MEL   But younger employees can. Younger, single employees. They're the most flexible.

DORIS   But what about all the years of loyalty, the years of acquiring company knowledge, doesn't that count for anything?

MEL   *(with total lack of emotion)* Not really. It's a disposable world in banking now. No-one expects their staff to stay longer than six years, at the most. They want to get the maximum amount of flexibility out of them while they are with the company. Having years of company knowledge counts for nothing when the knowledge is constantly changing. Each year there are new regulations, new ways of doing things, new marketing techniques, new markets, new products. What you learnt as an employee twenty years ago is completely valueless today. Sorry to be brutal.

DORIS   *(crumbling under the weight of unfairness)* That's what it is. It's brutal. It's morally indefensible. When I first went out to work you expected your employer to look after you. If you did a good job you got the perks. You got the pension plan...mind you, they didn't let the women in on that until the government forced them to...you got the sports club and the discounts on things. Now they've all been taken away, bit by bit, until we have nothing left. No security, no pride, no morale.

ETHAN	*(suddenly decisive)* I'm going to start looking for another job tomorrow. Not going to wait for the team to be broken up.
	(PATRICK returns with three cups of coffee and a bottle of water on a tray. He also has a cheese roll in his mouth. He hands out the coffee and the water and sits back down with his own cup.)
PATRICK	*(retrieving the roll from his mouth)* Well, have we progressed while I've been gone?
DORIS	*(very bitter)* No we haven't.
MEL	*(admonishing PATRICK)* You opened a whole can of worms, you did.
PATRICK	Me? What did I do?
MEL	All that nonsense about this being a management test and everything. Doris is upset and so is Ethan.
PATRICK	What about? I was only joking?
ETHAN	*(anguished)* They're selling the sports club, man!
PATRICK	*(surprised)* Didn't you know?
ETHAN	No I didn't. Changes everything.
PATRICK	I see. And what are you upset about Doris?
	(DORIS suddenly bursts into tears.)
DORIS	I...I don't want to retire! I want to work...I need to work! I can't stay at home and do nothing, I can't! It's so unfair!
MEL	*(getting up to comfort her)* But you don't have to retire. This early retirement package isn't compulsory. Nobody's going to force you to leave if you don't want to.
DORIS	*(broken-hearted)* But what's the point in staying? I'm just

surrounded by youngsters. Everyone I started with in this place has either left or is going to leave or has died. I feel like a foreigner in this place. I don't understand any of the management systems, I don't want to be constantly trained and retrained...I just want to do my job. I just want to let people draw out their money and pay money in. I don't want to try and sell pensions or insurance to everybody who comes up to my till. They hate it, you know. The customers hate it. And I just want to be able to talk to colleagues around me who understand what I'm talking about. I can't relate to anybody anymore. It's like being at school again and people saying "you can't belong to our gang, we don't like you" – it's horrible.

PATRICK   *(jovially)* What's wrong with taking early retirement? I think it's great. Bit of a financial pinch but not that much. And *you've* only got yourself to think about. You could do all sorts of things with your time. If you really wanted to work, though God knows why, do some voluntary stuff. Voluntary organizations are crying out for people like you, who are a whizz at organization.

DORIS   *(this makes her stop and think)* I suppose.

MEL   I think it would be the best thing, if you're so unhappy here.

DORIS   *(envious)* Well, it's alright for you. You understand what they want. I don't anymore. You know all the buzzwords – all the jargon. You make the right impression and you've got a great career ahead of you.

MEL   *(dismissive)* Thanks but I won't stay here for much longer.

PATRICK   *(amazed)* Good God! Why ever not?

MEL   *(scornful)* Huh! You wouldn't catch me working for this lot.
               Very poor management structure and very bad lines of
               communication. No, I'm just here for the training and then
               I'm off. Into consultancy where I can tell the likes of this
               bunch of dickheads how to improve their management
               strategy.

PATRICK   *(laughs loudly)* Hah! I love it! So, here we are. Four people,
               thoroughly disillusioned with the company, trying to
               organize a company PR event. You have to laugh!

               (Everyone starts laughing gently at the irony of it all.)

DORIS   It is ridiculous isn't it?

MEL   Absolutely.

ETHAN   Do we have to do it then?

MEL   Of course we do! Don't let the buggers grind you down.
               Give it your best shot and go out on a high. Come on,
               we've got fifteen minutes to wrap this quiz up! Let's get a
               move on. Doris, what's next?

DORIS   *(wiping her eyes, blowing her nose and gathering up her
               file again)* OK. So far we've got Ethan doing the Sports
               round, Mel, you're doing the "Most likely to say" round,
               Patrick, can you compile the General Knowledge questions?
               (He looks doubtful) Come on! You've only got to get them
               out of a book! I've got a couple here. *(She gets up and
               hands them to him)*

PATRICK   *(grudgingly)* OK. I'll do the General Knowledge round.

DORIS   Right. What are we going to have in the place of British
               history?

MEL   Have you got a TV round?

DORIS	Yes, that's round number nine.
ETHAN	*(eager)* Oh, can I do that one as well? I know loads about TV.
DORIS	Fine. I'll just write that down. Actually, it's TV and film. Still want to do it?
MEL	Why not split the two? Have one round about films and one round about TV?
DORIS	What, films could go in place of British history?
MEL	Yes.
ETHAN	*(enthusiastic)* Can I do that as well? I'm shit-hot on films as well.
DORIS	Fine. So Ethan's now doing three rounds – Sport, Television and Film. I think that's probably enough for him, don't you?
ETHAN	*(restless)* Yeah. Can I go now? Only I need to phone round the lads. We need to have a meeting about the club being sold off. We need to make plans, like.
DORIS	I don't see why not. Does anybody else mind? *(MEL and PATRICK murmur "no")* But I need those questions by the end of the week, remember, or I'll be chasing you.
ETHAN	Yeah. No problem. I won't let you down. Thanks.
MEL	*(warning him)* Er…Ethan…don't make loads of phone calls on the company phone. They're really clamping down on that.
ETHAN	No. It's OK. I'll use my mobile. I've got ten minutes before the doors open.
MEL	OK.

(ETHAN rushes out.)

DORIS	Poor Ethan. He's a nice boy. A bit dim but he's willing.
MEL	Yes. I'm sure he'll find another job. Now, let's crack on with this quiz.
DORIS	*(briskly)* OK. Let's recap. Round one – General Knowledge – Patrick to do. Round two – Sport – Ethan to do. Round three – Now films – Ethan to do. Round four – Food – Mel to do. Round five – Who is most likely to say? – Mel to do.
MEL	*(writing)* Got it. Round six?
DORIS	Round six is…or has always been…Geography.
MEL	Mmm. Make it Travel and we can relate it to the youngsters better.
PATRICK	*(dryly)* What, like "how many bars are there on the seafront at Benidorm?"
MEL	Very droll. I was thinking more like "how many hours does it take to fly to Greece?" That sort of thing. What do you think?
DORIS	*(becoming dismissive)* Don't look at me. I don't think I care anymore. If that's what you think will work, then you'd better do that round.
MEL	Fine by me.
DORIS	I still think it's pandering, though.
PATRICK	I thought you didn't care.
DORIS	I'm not sure, if I was honest, that I can totally give up a sense of pride in my work.
MEL	Isn't there a break before round six?
DORIS	Yes. The supper break.

MEL   Oh yes. Last year that was a cold buffet wasn't it?

DORIS   Yes. Is there anything wrong with that?

MEL   Well, I thought the food was a bit tired by that time in the evening. You know, sandwiches a bit dry and so on.

PATRICK   I agree. The catering staff make them in the morning and by the time it gets to nine in the evening it's not very good.

DORIS   Well, they cover them in clingfilm and refrigerate them!

MEL   Mmm. I think people would rather have something hot…in a basket, say.

DORIS   But that means that the catering staff will have to cook in the evening! They won't like that. Most of them come to the quiz night to relax.

MEL   *(delicately dropping another bombshell)* Well, actually, by the time we get to June, the catering staff will have been re-employed by an outside catering company. The management has decided to outsource that particular function.

(DORIS snaps her file shut in exasperation and looks irritable.)

DORIS   Whatever next! I suppose it will be burgers, pizzas and chips from now on then.

MEL   There'll be a large vegetarian section as well. A lot of our staff are vegetarians – particularly the Asian staff.

PATRICK   *(hopefully)* Oh, so we might get some nice curries then?

MEL   Probably.

DORIS   *(stating the obvious)* But no more roasts. No more shepherds pie. No more rice pudding.

MEL	No.
DORIS	*(depressed)* I've always relied on a substantial lunch, so that I didn't have to bother to cook when I got home.
MEL	You could always go out to a restaurant at lunchtime.
DORIS	*(shocked)* What at their prices! One of the good things about the staff cafeteria is the fact that it's subsidized.
MEL	Ah well it won't be any more.
DORIS and PATRICK	*(outraged)* What! No! etc.
MEL	*(holding up her hand to stifle the protests)* The prices will be reasonable but in line with commercial tariffs.
PATRICK	*(annoyed)* Damn! I'll have to get the wife to make me sandwiches every day.
MEL	So. By June, as I said, we should be able to offer a full cafeteria service for the quiz night.
DORIS	Won't that take a long time to serve? I mean the break is only supposed to be half an hour.
MEL	Mr Jenkins thought that it would be better to make it an hour, then we could sell more raffle tickets.
DORIS	*(coldly angry)* Oh he did, did he? Why didn't Mr Jenkins tell me all of this?
MEL	I couldn't say.
DORIS	*(seething)* Right. Well round seven can be scrapped then.
MEL	*(genuinely puzzled)* Sorry?
DORIS	*(being vindictive)* Round seven has always been about American history – by special request of Mr Jenkins because

he likes showing off his encyclopedic knowledge of everything to do with America. No-one else knows the answers to the questions and they've always moaned about it. I'll be buggered if I'm going to include it this year as Mr Jenkins hasn't seen fit to tell me about all the changes in procedure.

MEL   *(shrugging)* No skin of my nose. Patrick?

PATRICK   As long as Doris is the one to tell him that it's been scrapped, I couldn't give a stuff.

DORIS   I shall take great pleasure in doing so, believe me.

MEL   *(smiling)* You know, when I came here, you were so slavishly devoted to Mr Jenkins I thought that you and he were...

DORIS   *(sharply)* What?

MEL   *(smiling)* You know. I thought you were banging the boss.

DORIS   *(appalled)* Good God! That's disgusting!

MEL   Sorry. Should have put it more delicately.

DORIS   No, I mean that you should even think such a thing! I was just taught that, as an employee, you showed utter loyalty to your boss. That's all. Good God!

MEL   Oh I know. I realized that when I found out that he'd been having an affair with Sally from Business Banking for years.

DORIS   *(even more appalled)* What!

PATRICK   *(amiably)* Oh that only started about five years ago. It was Celia Parker before that.

MEL   Who's she?

PATRICK   She left under mysterious circumstances. She probably took it all too seriously and wanted him to leave his wife or something.

MEL   *(suddenly noticing that DORIS has become very quiet and distracted)* Ah. Are you alright Doris?

(DORIS is sitting in stunned silence, looking stricken.)

MEL   Doris?

DORIS   *(speaking as if to herself)* Yes. Yes. I'm fine. It's just a shock, that's all. You think you know someone. You work for them for twenty years and it turns out you don't know them at all. *(Pulling herself together)* Right. Round seven. What shall we have? I know. Birds.

MEL   Birds?

DORIS   Yes the feathered kind. One subject that Jenkins knows absolutely nothing about.

PATRICK   But will anyone else?

DORIS   *(viciously)* Tough. There has to be one round that's more challenging than a children's television programme.

MEL   OK. Birds. Who's going to compile it?

DORIS   Me.

MEL   Fine. What's next?

DORIS   Round nine is taken care of. Ethan's doing TV. Round ten has always been Anagrams.

MEL   What? Jumbled up letters?

DORIS   *(smiling in a vindictive way)* Yes, as in – *(she furiously writes some letters down on her pad and hands them to MEL)*

MEL   *(Reading the letters out)* H T I S G I Y N L E T I T L L.

	What does that make?
DORIS	Mr Jenkins.
MEL	*(frowning)* I can't see that. There's no J and there's no K.
DORIS	*(slightly hysterical)* If you unscramble the letters it says "Lying little shit".
MEL	*(sighing)* Right. Have you lost the will to do this quiz, Doris?
DORIS	*(embarrassed)* No, sorry. I was just being childish.
MEL	*(firmly)* I think we'll scrap Anagrams and go for something more relevant.
PATRICK	*(actually having an idea)* How about picking a decade?
MEL	Good idea. Lets make it the 1980's. Got that Doris?
DORIS	Yes. I'm just writing it down. You'll have to compile that one.
MEL	Fine. So I'm doing food, Who is most likely to say?, travel and the 1980's. Ethan is doing sport, TV and films. Doris is doing birds and Patrick, you're doing General Knowledge. That leaves one more round. Doris?
DORIS	It's always been a music round. You know, we play pieces of music and they have to name the composer or singer.
MEL	That's fine, as long as we make it a mix of music, not all classical or old stuff.
DORIS	I'm sorry to say this Mel, but if you want current music then you're going to have to compile yet another round yourself.
MEL	*(shrugs)* Doesn't bother me. I've got millions of CD's. I can

cobble something together really quickly.

DORIS   *(hesitantly)* Patrick and I are only doing one round each.

PATRICK   Don't complain old girl! Suits me fine.

DORIS   *(annoyed)* Well it would suit you but it doesn't suit me. I feel I should contribute more.

MEL   Well let's leave the raffle entirely up to you, shall we? You can organize the prizes and the tickets and everything.

DORIS   *(relieved)* That's fine. I'm happy doing that. Well, that seems to be it. I'll type up all the categories and take them into Jenkins later.

MEL   I can do it if you like.

DORIS   *(coldly)* No. I have to see him anyway. I need to tell him that I'm accepting the early retirement package. The sooner the better, frankly.

MEL   I'm sure you're making a wise decision.

DORIS   *(bitter once more)* But I'm not making the decision, am I? It's really been made for me. The rug's been pulled out from under me and I have no choice but to fall. Anyway, I'll get on with all this and see you later. Bye.

               (DORIS leaves – a very much diminished figure from the woman that came into the meeting room. There is a brief silence while MEL makes a few notes and PATRICK just looks at her.)

PATRICK   *(slyly)* Well. You've achieved what you wanted to achieve.

MEL   Yes. Thank you for playing your part. *(She takes an envelope out of her pocket and hands it to him)* You'll find a new contract of employment in there which gives you another two years with the bank. You'll finish the week after the mortgage on your house is paid off.

PATRICK   *(he puts the envelope in his jacket pocket)* Thank you. It will make life a little easier. *(He feels a little remorseful)* Was it really necessary for Doris to go?

MEL   *(matter-of-factly)* Yes. Apart from the fact that she is occupying a valuable supervisor's job, she was becoming a liability. She had started criticising the bank's policies in front of the customers.

PATRICK   *(sly again)* Agreeing with the customer's complaints you mean?

MEL   *(unbothered by his remark)* If you like. But you know that that is not something that you do. You have to present a united front to the outside world.

PATRICK   *(probing)* Of course. And Ethan? Was it necessary for him to go, as well?

MEL   *(being frank)* Yes. He wasn't up to the job but we don't like to sack teenagers, it looks bad on their CV's. It's better if he goes of his own accord.

PATRICK   We? You said we.

MEL   I meant the bank.

PATRICK   Of course – but then you *are* the bank.

MEL   *(detecting an implied insult)* I beg your pardon?

PATRICK   A perfect representation of the bank. Ambitious, ruthless, calculating. *(admiring but revolted at the same time)* You're some piece of work.

MEL   *(becoming officious)* I don't think you are in a position to criticize me. After all, you played no small part in today's exercise.

PATRICK   *(sighing)* I should be ashamed of myself but I've always been a selfish bugger. God knows I don't want to work in this place but I need to pay off that mortgage before I cut the old umbilical cord. Was it necessary to be so hard on her?

MEL   Doris? It was necessary to get rid of her motivation to work here. Yes. It was the only way.

PATRICK   I suppose your degree, the one that you worked so hard for, was in psychology.

MEL   Correct.

PATRICK   *(probing slyly again)* Will Mr Jenkins be happy with what you've achieved today?

MEL   Of course.

PATRICK   And you will be promoted.

MEL   *(smiling to herself)* Whether or not I'm promoted has nothing to do with Mr Jenkins. He won't be around for much longer anyway.

PATRICK   *(amused)* Ha! Like I said, you are some piece of work. You know all the right buttons to push. You knew I was lazy and greedy the moment you laid eyes on me. You knew that Doris had to have her heart broken and her beliefs shattered before she would leave this bank and you knew that Ethan only cared about his sport. So, what, I wonder, have you got on old Jenkins. My God there must be so many things! A vain, pompous womanizer like that! I'd love to know when your axe is going to fall on him.

MEL   You know, Patrick. You are really very intelligent. It's such a pity you're so lazy. However, I'm sure I shall find you very useful over the next two years. Particularly at the Quiz Night.

PATRICK   *(genuinely puzzled)* The Quiz Night?

MEL   *(smoothly)* Yes. I have a very special friend coming to the Quiz Night. Only I don't want it known that she is my friend. I'd like her to be *your* friend for that evening and I'd like you to introduce her to Mr Jenkins.

PATRICK   *(enjoying the conspiracy)* Let me guess. She wouldn't happen to be a very good-looking blonde, would she? Only you do know that old Jenkins only likes blondes.

MEL   Oh yes. She's very good-looking and very blonde. She's also very clever and very expensive.

PATRICK   *(nodding and smiling)* And all I have to do is introduce her to Jenkins?

MEL   That's all you have to do.

PATRICK   And do I get anything for this service?

MEL   *(suddenly becoming very tough)* You get that contract in your pocket guaranteed, even if a whole new management structure takes over.

PATRICK   *(suddenly unnerved)* Fine. That's absolutely fine. *(He gets up to go)* Is there anything else I should do?

MEL   *(speaking to him over her shoulder, without looking at him)*

Yes. I suggest that you consider, along with everyone else who presently works at this bank, signing up for evening classes in Chinese.

PATRICK   *(looking aghast)* Jesus!

BLACKOUT.

FURNITURE LIST

Throughout: Five matching occasional chairs (plastic or chrome office-type furniture); either four small matching glass or formica tables or one large coffee table (again, office-type furniture); filing cabinet (or a good substitute for this would be a flip chart on an easel); potted plants; bank posters on the wall (or sales charts etc.); other set-dressing as appropriate.

PROPERTY LIST

Page 1:   DORIS: enters with a file/organiser, containing various papers and pens; polystyrene cup of coffee.

MEL: enters with a notepad and pen and an envelope in her pocket (required for the end of the play – not visible now).

Page 2:   ETHAN: enters with a polystyrene cup of coffee.

Page 4:   DORIS: hands out two sheets of questions.

Page 6:   PATRICK: enters with a polystyrene cup of coffee; a Danish Pastry wrapped in clingfilm.

Page 15:   PATRICK: enters with a tray of three polystyrene cups of coffee and a bottle of mineral water, with a cheese roll in his mouth.

LIGHTING AND EFFECTS PLOT

Music beginning and end.

Page 1:   switch the lights on. (Normal range of stage lights for
                   interior, day)

Page 29:   switch the lights off.

No sound effects.